MEDITACIÓN
FRONTERIZA

Camino del Sol

A Latina and Latino Literary Series

NORMA ELIA CANTÚ

MEDITACIÓN FRONTERIZA

Poems of Love, Life, and Labor

THE UNIVERSITY OF
ARIZONA PRESS

TUCSON

The University of Arizona Press
www.uapress.arizona.edu

© 2019 by Norma Elia Cantú
All rights reserved. Published 2019

ISBN-13: 978-0-8165-3935-2 (paper)

Cover design by Leigh McDonald
Cover art: *La Pisca* by Natalia Anciso

Publication of this book is made possible in part by the proceeds of a permanent endowment created
with the assistance of a Challenge Grant from the National Endowment for the Humanities, a federal
agency.

Library of Congress Cataloging-in-Publication Data are available at the Library of Congress.

Printed in the United States of America
♾ This paper meets the requirements of ANSI/NISO Z39.48-1992 (Permanence of Paper).

Love is social movement, and enacted by revolutionary, mobile, and global coalitions of citizen-activists who are allied though the apparatus of emancipation.

—CHELA SANDOVAL

The U.S.-Mexican border es una herida abierta where the Third World grates against the first and bleeds. And before a scab forms it hemorrhages again, the lifeblood of two worlds merging to form a third country—a border culture.

—GLORIA EVANGELINA ANZALDÚA

No one who survives to speak
new language, has avoided this:
the cutting away of an old force that held her
rooted to an old ground.

—ADRIENNE RICH

CONTENTS

V. GOING HOME

VI. MEDITACIÓN FRONTERIZA

¡GRACIAS!

FRIENDS, FAMILY, AND FELLOW POETS helped birth this collection with their support and gifts of time and wisdom. I thank you all:

Sandra Cisneros and Claire Joysmith generously commented on a very early draft. ¡Gracias, Sandra and Claire!

The border scholar Socorro Tabuenca read an earlier version of this final manuscript. ¡Gracias, Coquis! ire'ne lara silva pored over the final version. ¡Gracias, amiga!

Elvia and Elsa, my supporters and cheerleaders, offered invaluable assistance at various points. Thank you for giving me the space to do the work. ¡Mil gracias!

To the poets of CantoMundo who heard me read some of these poems and to all wordsmiths who have honored me with their friendship, my eternal gratitude. ¡Gracias!

Finally, to the Creator who guides my every step: ¡Gracias!

Some of the poems in *Meditación fronteriza* have been previously published, sometimes in slightly different versions or with different titles: "Canto a la tierra fronteriza" and "Capricho" in *Hinchas de Poesía*; "She Was a Bobolo Grandmother" in *Kweli Journal*; "La luna" (stanza VI in "Trying to Be"), "Sangre en el desierto" (stanza I in "Border Triptych"), and "Two Countries" (stanza II in "Border Triptych") in *Sonarida: Revista de Encuentro entre Sonora y Arizona*; "La luna," "Sangre en el desierto," and "Two Countries" in *Puentes: Revista méxico-chicana de literaria, cultura y arte*; "Border Bullets" and "The Body/My Body" in *Chicana/Latina Studies: The Journal of Mujeres Activas en Letras y Cambio Social*; "The Killing Path" and "In the Country of Art" in *Voices de la Luna*; "Song of the Borderlands," "Miel de mesquite," and "A Sor Juana" in *riverSedge*; "The Wall" in *Vandal*; "Reading the Body" and "Migraine" in *Telling to Live: Latina Feminist Testimonios*; "Decolonizing the Mind" in *Cantar de espejos: Poesía testimonial chicana de mujeres*; "La Llorona Considers the State of Tortillas" in *Feminist Studies* (reprinted in *Poetic Voices Without Borders 2*, edited by Robert L. Girón); and "Meditación fronteriza I, II, and III" in *Acentos Review*. Excerpts of some poems appear in artwork by Marta Sánchez and in our book *Transcendental Train Yard*.

MEDITACIÓN FRONTERIZA

I

SONG OF THE BORDERLANDS

CANTO A LA TIERRA FRONTERIZA

Es mi tierra fronteriza
    pedazo de mi corazón
tierra donde los Carrizo
los Comecrudo, los Coahuiltecos
    cruzaban ríos
        festejaban la primavera
            sufrían inviernos
vivían   morían

Con pieles de liebre cobijaban a sus niños
    tomaban el agua clara del río
        cazaban venado, jabalí
            cosechaban mesquites y tunas del nopal
vivían   morían

Es mi tierra fronteriza,
tierra de mis antepasados—
    mamagrande, papagrande
        Bueli, Güelito—
tierra donde
    abuelas y abuelos
        bisabuelos y tatarabuelas
vivían   morían

Aquí enterraron mi ombligo en un día sábado de enero
    al anochecer debajo del pirul
        aquí enterraron a mis muertitos
            mis primeras sangres

En esta tierra fronteriza
               nacieron mis primeros anhelos
                    mis primeros instintos, deseos,
                        mis primeras añoranzas
                  aquí mis sueños
     vivían   morían

Es mi tierra fronteriza where all my relations
    breathed the morning air heavy with dew
             neblina que purifica with sage smoke
                   in a sunrise ceremony
                     early morning sweeping the yard
regando las plantas al amanecer

En mi tierra fronteriza
    los gallos le cantan al amanecer
             y el cascabeleo de las víboras se escurre en mi
                 aquí las víboras viven y mueren
como cualesquiera que nace en este lugar
áspero y rudo—tierno como el nopalito
en Cuaresma

Es mi tierra fronteriza
    donde me quedo hasta que se llegue
            la hora de mi muerte
                  muerte al fin encadenada a la vida
            muerte que nutre el vivir de cada día
    muerte que no es más que renacer de primavera,
mesquite bañado en florecillas amarillas

SONG OF THE BORDERLAND[*]

My land is a borderland
   piece of my heart
land where the Carrizo,
Comecrudos, the Coahuiltecos
   crossed rivers
         celebrated spring
            suffered winter
they lived   they died

They birthed babies
   cradled them, warmed by the pelt of young rabbits
      drank clear waters from the river
         hunted the deer and jabalí
           picked mesquites and tunas
lived   died

My land is a borderland
the land of my antepasados—
   mamagrande, papagrande,
      Bueli, Güelito—
Land where grandparents,
   great-grandparents,
      great-great-grandparents
ancestors all
lived   died

---

[*]   Translated by the author.

Here they buried my afterbirth
    one Saturday in January
            at dusk beneath the willow
                    Here lie my dead ones, my buried
                    first bloods

My land is a borderland
nurturing my first yearnings
    my first instincts, desires
            my first longings
                    Here my dreams
lived   died

My land is a borderland
donde mis antepasados vivían y morían
    purifying early morning dew con humo de cenizo
            en la ceremonia al amanecer
                    por la mañana barriendo el jardín
                    watering the garden at sunrise

My land is a borderland
    where roosters sing at dawn
            the rattlesnake molts
its rattling seeping into me
    from first to last breath
                    like all who are born on this rude land
            land tender as the prickly pear
                    during Lent

My land is a borderland
    where I shall remain until
            the hour of my death
                    death in the end, linked to life
    death that is nothing more than spring's rebirth
mesquite tree bathed in yellow blossoming

SHE WAS A BOBOLO GRANDMOTHER

She was a Bobolo grandmother
en el Nuevo Santander
who in her grief self-immolated
like the Vietnamese monks and nuns.
But in the 1700s, no TV camera recorded
her death at her own hands,
protesting the invasion.

The Spanish took it as proof of
the savagery, the inhumanity.
The others, her own people,
wanted her to succumb,
to give in. Pretend to believe in the foreign god.

But her grandchild laid dead.
The tall foreign soldier had taken the infant
from her daughter,
smashed the tiny piece of her heart
against a tree, then raped her daughter.
How could she
live in a world where
such things happened?

So she set herself afire
calmly sitting at the very spot that would become
the center of the town in the plaza of that river
town in Nuevo Santander,
the flames burning all her pain and hate.

No marker honors her death
and no one knows her name,
but the historian chronicled her death,
and thereby she lives.

HABLANDO Y SOÑANDO

"Me siento como un río subterráneo entre la piel y la realidad, mis aguas son mis versos que humedecen el desierto del alma".

—CARMEN VASCONES

En el rió muere otro hombre. Ahogado.
Por eso hemos venido hasta aquí.
Y siento un río que me instiga llanto y gemidos profundos
que me mueve hacia un fin determinado por la luna
o el sol de mediodía
desde un lado hacia el otro.
Un río. La corriente fuerte de primavera,
la sangre me hace cosquillas con sus remolinos
al correr por mis venas.

¡Lo que hemos tenido que dejar para llegar hasta aquí!

Muñecas de trapo, mi colección de LPs de los 60s, los CDs de los 90s,
    el barrio de mi niñez, las cartas, tus cartas de amor, depresión aguda
    y profunda como la noche, la solidez de la casa materna, ilusiones
    de paz, de alegría, Che Guevara, el Marxismo, mis ideas de justicia,
    la iglesia de mi niñez con sus flores de mayo, y todo lo que cargaba
    a cuestas desde la Guerra que aún no termina.

Esa Guerra.

Y hemos venido hasta aquí,
por eso que fuimos y jamás volveremos a ser.
Platicamos toda la noche de lo que no pudo ser
y lo que tal vez será.

Lo que fué: comidas en
México Típico en Nuevo Laredo,

Rosita's en Laredo
Lhardy en Madrid
Mi Tierra en San Antonio,
paseos por el Retiro o el River Walk, da igual.

Te tomo la mano y me estremezco.
Fantasma de mi juventud.
In lak'ech: tú eres mi otro yo, "my impossible spouse."
Llegamos hasta este lugar de llanto, de escombros.
Queremos cambiarlo todo, pasear entre
jardines de suculentos verde-oscuros,
a las orillas del río, entre muros de carrizo, de hierbas.
Envueltos en silencio los árboles:
'nacahuitas, mesquites, huisaches
y algún palo verde o retama por ahí.
Los arboles sueñan, se mecen con el vaivén
del viento. Murmuran sus secretos.
Cuánto no habrán visto, testigos del dolor y del amor.
Llegamos a donde tenemos que llegar.

Aquí nos enfrentamos con él.
Me cree inútil contigo o sin ti.
Nos advierte: hay peligro.
Enumera los riesgos;
platicamos un rato.
"Los que cruzan saben bien a lo que se atienen
pero se arriesgan igual,
se cuidan unos a los otros,
pero al final cada quien viene solo."

Te miro y me hundo en tus ojos profundos
como de luto.
Tu dolor y tu ser palpable como el lodo en este río.
tus ojos me cuentan historias desconocidas, de siempre.

Hablamos de lo que fue y de lo que será
como si con el hecho de hablarlas
las palabras se convirtieran en verdad
como que probáramos ser dioses, creadores del futuro
diosas que amadran el futuro.

Te aseguro: en el río viven mundos ajenos
con dioses propios.
¿No me crees? ¿No me entiendes?

Que triste vivir sin fe,
con solo las palabras para sentirse fiel,
solo la ciencia para cerciorar la realidad,
seguir por el mundo sin mirar atrás,
sin añorar lo que fue, sin soñar con lo que podría ser.

TALKING   DREAMING†

"I feel an underground river between skin and reality, my waters are my poems that dampen the desert that is my soul."

—CARMEN VASCONES

In the river another man dies. Drowned.
That is why we have come.
I feel a river that impels, weeping, deep wailing
moving me toward an end set by the moon
or the noontime sun
from one side to the other.
A river. A strong spring current
the blood tickles me with its
eddies as it runs through my veins.

What we've had to leave behind to get here!

Rag dolls, my LP collection from the '60s, my CDs from the '90s,
    my childhood barrio, my letters, your love letters, acute depression
    deep as night, the solid base of my parents' home, illusions of peace,
    of joy, Che Guevara, Marxism, my ideas of justice, my childhood
    church with its May flowers, and all that I carried on my back since
    the War, that War that will not end. That War.

And we have come to this place
because of what we were and will never be again.
We chat all night about what can never be,
of what was and what will be, perhaps.

What was: meals at
México Típico en Nuevo Laredo

---

†   Translated by the author.

Rosita's in Laredo
Lhardy in Madrid
Mi Tierra in San Antonio,
long walks through el Retiro
or San Antonio's River Walk, it's all the same.

I take your hand and I tremble.
Ghost of my youth.
In lak'ech. You are my other I, "mi pareja imposible."
We arrive to this place of tears, of ruins.
We want to change it all, take our walks amidst
succulent dark green gardens,
at the river's edge between walls of reeds and weeds.
Shrouded by the trees' silences:
'nacahuitas, mesquites, huisaches,
perhaps a palo verde or retama along the way–
Trees dream, they swing with the rhythm
of the wind. They whisper their secrets.
How much they have seen, witnesses to pain and love.
We arrive where we must.

We meet him.
He believes me to be useless with or without you.
He warns us: there is danger.
He lists the risks.
We talk a bit.
"Those who cross know well what they face,
but they take the risk, nonetheless.
They care for one another,
but in the end each one comes alone."

I look at you and I sink in the depths of your eyes,
eyes like mourning.
Your pain and your being as thick as the mud in the river.
Your eyes tell me unknown stories. Stories of always.

We talk about what was and what will be,
as if saying the words would make the words real,
as if we had tried at being gods, creators of the future.

I assure you: in the river live alien worlds
with their own gods.
You don't believe me? You don't understand me?

How sad it must be to live without faith,
with only words to make one feel faithful,
with only science to hold up what is reality,
to go through this world without looking back,
without yearning for what was, without dreaming of what could be.

TRATANDO DE SER

I

En la frontera truenos y relámpagos
me hieren hasta el alma.
A veces siento que el río
se me impone.
Ese rio casi Bravo y no muy Grande
que se ríe de la gente con mueca de
calavera de Halloween—¡o de Catrina!
"Como se ve tan mansito,
la gente se atreve a cruzarlo".

II

Cuando lleguemos,
nomás pasando el desierto,
hasta ese mundo de Disney,
hasta ese lugar de fábricas
y trabajos bien pagados,
cuando lleguemos,
entonces seremos felices.
Seremos lo que somos,
si nos dejan.

III

Envueltos en silencio
nos cobijamos con la noche

y con las sombras.
Es un atardecer como cualquier otro,
con la luz del ocaso
brindando el primer lucero que se asoma
como en canción de cuna.
Y yo me siento aún más inútil
ante la realidad de la oscuridad.
Tú, ¿qué dices?
Tu mirada recita versos
de Neruda.
Me cubres con tu aliento,
y el peligro ya no existe.
Aun, tienes miedo, lo huelo.

Hablamos de cómo es que llegamos aquí.
Tú, sin tener vela en el entierro,
vienes acompañándome
en esta, mi tarea de nómada;
por medio mundo me has seguido,
sin la necesidad.
Sedienta de otros aires.
Tú sabes lo que menos temo.
Y conoces todos mis achaques,
igual que mis antojos.

IV

Cómo decirte que ya no soy la que fui,
cómo explicarte que nosotras mismas no somos aquellas,
cómo demostrarte que ni tú ni yo sabemos nada de esta vida.
¿Qué piensas? ¿No me entiendes?

No se cómo ser la que fui,
aquella la que se quedó en el río,

cuyo nombre no recuerdo,
esa ya no existe.
Ahora soy yo quien
prefiere no ir de compras, no comer en restaurán,
no hablar de inanidades.
Y tú, ¿qué quieres?

V

Ya no soy la que fui,
aquella que creía en la vida,
la que moría por el dolor de los demás.
Y tú, ya no eres la de antes,
ahora me miras con lástima,
no con adoración.
¿De dónde vienen los sueños?
¿A dónde nos llevan los suspiros?
¿Qué quieres?
¿Qué quiero?
¿A quién amamos como a nosotras mismas?

VI

Luz de luna,
guardián que vigilas,
luna guerrillera,
te pedimos.
Te rogamos.
¡Aligera el dolor con tu luz,
Coyolxauhqui!
Ayúdanos a recordar
el yo verdadero.
¡Gracias!

TRYING TO BE[‡]

I

On the border thunder and lightning
hurt me to my very soul.
Sometimes I feel the river
forces itself upon me.
That river almost Bravo and not too Grande
a river that laughs at people with a
Halloween skull grin—or like a Catrina's!
"Since it appears so tame,
people dare to cross it."

II

When we arrive,
as soon as we cross the desert
toward Disney's world,
toward that place of factories
and well-paid jobs,
when we arrive,
then, we will be happy.
We will be who we are
if they let us.

[‡]   Translated by the author.

III

Wrapped in silence,
we lay covered by night
and by shadows.
It's a sunset like any other
with the light of dusk
offering the first star that peeks
like in a lullaby,
and I feel even more helpless
at the reality of darkness.
What do you say?
Your look recites poems
by Neruda.
Your breath covers me
and danger ceases to exist.
Yet you fear, I can smell it.

We talk of how we got here.
You have no reason to be here.
You've come to keep me company
on this, my nomad's task.

Through half a world you have followed me
without a thirst for other climates.
You know what I least fear.
And you know all my aches
and all my yearnings.

IV

How can I tell you I am no longer who I was?
How to explain that we are not the same?
How to show you that neither you nor I

know anything about this life?
What do you think? Don't you understand?

I do not know how to be who I was,
she who remained in the river,
whose name I cannot recall;
she no longer exists.
Now it is I who
prefers not to go shopping,
not to dine in restaurants,
not to talk about inane things.
And you, what do you want?

V

I am no longer who I was,
she who believed in life,
who died with the pain of others.
And you are no longer the one you were.
Now you see me with pity.
Not with adoring eyes.
Where do dreams come from?
Where do sighs take us? What do you want?
What do I want?
Whom do we love like we love ourselves?

VI

Moonlight,
vigilant guardian,
warrior moon,
we ask.
We plead.

Soften the pain with your light,
Coyolxauhqui!
Help us remember
our true selves.
¡Gracias!

BORDER BULLETS

Rio Grande flows
from the Rockies to the Gulf
holy waters heal the border scar
pecan, nogal, retama sway,
tower o'er mesquites, huisaches
buried treasure brown

fiery gold crown
sun sets over Mexico
death defies life
a packed train speeds by
transports precious cargo
arrives with the moonlight

THE KILLING PATH

They travel the path cautiously,
careful and watchful,
watching out for la migra,
those who will catch and send
without remorse.

They travel the path hopefully,
hopeful and faithful,
trusting that at the other end
food, drink, clean clothes await,
the end where all will be well.

They travel the path faithfully
along a treacherous and onerous road.
They may regret the choice
but see no option except death,
slow and sure.

they travel the path
they travel the path
they travel

we travel the path
we travel the path
we travel

SONG OF THE BORDERLANDS

A poem for choral reading for three male voices (MV) and three female voices (FV)

ALL: We are descendants of proud

MALE VOICE #1: Mestizos

FEMALE VOICE #1: Españoles

MV #2 AND FV #2: Indios—

ALL: Coahuiltecos

MV #2: Carrizo

FV #2: Comecrudo

MV #3 AND FV #3: Lipan Apache

MV #2 AND FV#2: Karankahua

ALL: y tantos otros

FV #3: forgotten

FV #3 AND MV #2: yet all live in our blood

ALL: Will you forget us all?

MV #1: We ate corn and mesquite

FV #2: blossoms and roots

FV #3 AND MV #2: crossed the raging river

FV #1 AND MV #3: *(loud voice)* CROSSED THE RAGING RIVER

FV #2 AND MV #2: CROSSED THE RAGING RIVER

ALL: CROSSED THE RAGING RIVER

MV #3: suffered droughts and storms

FV #1: Snow fell on these lands back then

ALL: Will you forget us all?

FV #1: The Spanish captains

FV #3: and the lowly hired hands

MV #1: came trudging

MV #2 AND FV #1: conquering

MV #1 AND FV #2: suffering the heat

ALL: singing songs

MV #1: con guitarra y vihuela

FV #3: añoranzas of the faraway land

MV #2: naranjos en flor

FV #1: azahares y amapolas

MV #1, #2, AND #3: They came with Christian God

FV #1, #2, AND #3: and conquered all

MV #1: the land

FV #1: la tierra

MV #2: the language

FV #2: la lengua

MV #3: the people

FV #3: los pueblos

FV #1, #2, AND #3: We did not see that we became them

MV #1, #2, AND #3: and they did not see that they became us

ALL: Will you forget and let us go?

FV #1 AND #2: Over a hundred fifty years ago, the others came

MV #1 AND #3: the river became a wound and blood flooded

MV #1, #2, AND #3: Mestizos

FV #1, #2, AND #3: Mestizas

MV #1 AND FV #1: the label stuck to our foreheads

MV #2 AND FV #2: our lips learned to shape yet another language

MV #1, #2, AND #3: and they whipped us

FV #1, #2, AND #3: lynched us

ALL: because we were not them

MV #1, #2, AND #3: Will you forget us and never let us be?

FV #1, #2, AND #3: Will you never let us go?

FV #1, #2, AND #3: They came, ordered, and commanded

MV #1, #2, AND #3: From the North they came

MV #2: The trains came with roars of death

FV #1: came with steel crushing the wildflowers

MV #1: The river ran its course

MV #1 AND FV #1: We knew the truth and kept it

FV #1, #2, AND #3: (*whisper*) keep it

MV #1 AND #2: in our hearts

FV #1: The moon

FV #2 AND #3: la misma luna

FV #2 AND MV #2: bears witness—

FV #1 AND #3: (*whisper*) silent witness

MV #1: and the mesquite

FV #2: el huisache

MV #2: anacahuita

FV #3: el nopal

MV #3: and the yucca

FV #2 AND #3, MV #2 AND #3: el monte entero

ALL: (*loud voice*) NOS RECUERDA

MV #1 AND FV #2: that we are still here

MV #2 AND #3: still living

FV #2 AND #3: (*whisper*) still

ALL: You will never let us go

MV #1, #2, AND #3: let us be

FV #1, #2, AND #3: let us fly

MV #1, #2, AND #3: (*whisper*) We will always be

FV #1, #2, AND #3: (*normal voice*) We will always be

ALL: (*loud voice*) We will always be

ALL: (*Louder still. Pause between each word*) WE   WILL   ALWAYS   BE

ALL: (*repeat together*) We will always be!

We will always be!

BORDER TRIPTYCH

I

Sangre en el desierto
The strange fruit of the desert
Lies rotting in the sands of time
A shoe, a scarf, a thimble full of faith
Remains. The only trail worth dying for
Forgotten. From El Salvador
to México
to Texas
the dream deferred lies still
los restos finally at rest.

II

Two countries
Speaking
Both
Ambos idiomas,
Bartering in
Both
Pesos and dólares
Listening to
Both
Hip-hop y rancheras
Dancing to
Both

Cumbias and country
Saluting
Both
Ambas banderas

The red white and blue y la verde blanco y colorado
We are indios y europeos
We are güeros y prietos
We are fronterizos, mestizos
We are.

III

In the Valley, the river slithers
To the Gulf.
In this Coahuiltecan desert
The earth cries out.
With consuming hunger,
The zopilotes circle above
Gather   are sated.

TERRA INCOGNITA

I am like the mockingbird,
cenzontle of a thousand songs,
singing a welcome song
in the many languages of this land.

An unknown land that remains between—
Nepantla—frontera,
a land of drought and floods,
a land of death,
scorching heat,
sapping strength . . . life.

A land, life,
river water flowing,
watermelon ripening,
giving life and power.

This land that feeds the wild,
the untamed—
gato montes, jabalí, lagartijo,
the tamed—
cats, dogs, horses,
feeds us ALL, aquellos de ayer y de hoy
who dwell in the glow of
dusk and dawn.

This land once fed
Carrizos and Apaches,

gringos y gachupines,
igual que a tí y a mí
and other in-betweens.

And yet cuando crees que la conoces
this land turns on you,
reminding you that you don't know it at all.

The spirits of the land,
the flora and fauna,
the past and the now
could be friend or foe.

I am like the mockingbird,
cenzontle of a thousand songs,
singing a welcome song
in the many languages of this land,
yet I have no map to give you.
No soothing song
No peace to offer.

SOUTH TEXAS–JULY 2014

Yesterday, released to the surf
    in Port A
           the turtles, mere hatchlings.
    Someday they will return to this very shore.
    This Gulf.
           Following their own timing, they go, they come.

Yesterday, they kidnapped him.
    Today, murdered him. My friend's father.
    He was sixty-five. A loving father.
        A businessman.
            A husband.
            An uncle.
Now he is a statistic. What's left? A son, a widow.
A community grieving the loss. In pain.

The eleven- or fourteen-year-old boy from Honduras,
wearing Angry Birds pants,
    had his uncle's telephone
        number on his belt. The uncle in Chicago.
           They found the boy's decomposing body in the
           brush.
Alone.   He wandered off away from the others.
Lost.
    To die.
        Alone.

From such stuff nightmares. "Mi cariño huerfano de besos . . ."
The cotton plants, a green sea. Not yet ready, greet July, wait for
    August y sus capullos de algodon.
Who will be there to grieve?
Who? When all are dead or gone?
Who will release the hatchlings?
Will the turtles return to nothing?

THE WALL

Written on a visit to Nuevo Progreso, Tamaulipas, Méjico, May 15, 2009

No one believed it would happen here
en el Valle
where the birders find such joy
in spotting unique exotic birds.
No one believed they would build it here.
"Just talk," someone said,
"puro pedo.
Not to worry, they'll never get the money."

But the wall went up,
and hardly anyone noticed
the way the land was rent in two
the way the sky
above seemed bluer against the brown metal
jutting up and up and up
like soldiers saluting a distant god
sentinels silently guarding . . . what?

Perhaps a way of life
incongruent with their dreams,
a pastiche of broken people
crossing their quotidian desires
from one side to the other.

All legal and safe,
sipping margaritas en el mercado
or shopping at Walmart
living.

Best of both worlds,
a friend tells me. But you gotta be legal to live it.
Not for everyone the fruits of gringolandia.
Not everyone sees the wall.

Walls make good enemies: suspicious, defensive,
fearful, who hide behind a wall
solid as a heart hardened by fear.
Who would've believed it would happen here?

II

READING THE BODY

READING THE BODY

Start with a literal exegesis
and thereby refute all metaphor.
                    ¡calla boca!
The historical record reigns supreme:
battle scars, accidental burns, scraped-knee scars.
Surgeries: appendectomy, hysterectomy, mastectomy.

Birth marks destiny.
And I wonder at the state of limb and joint
at three. Thirteen. Thirty.
Examine teeth and hair to discern age;
look for skin's sun signs—spots and lines tell the tale—
palitos y bolitas uniquely etched.

Then consider metaphor—decipher choices
written in blood: children borne or not.
Breasts that suckled lovers/infants,
feet well-shod or well-heeled,
work-roughened or smoothly manicured hands,
nun's hands, ringed in gold.
Read the lessons of ages writ in parable
upon sagging flesh;
the seven ages (or nine lives) would speak tomes.

Finally, deconstruct
the gendered
racialized mind
in patterns, rich and plain

clearly stamped upon a haircut,
earringed lobe, nose or nipple,
tattoos, birthmarks.
Test the script
with the language of bones, of skin.

The body speaks in tongues
far more eloquent than mere words.
A flushed cheek, a sweaty palm,
the scent of menses and of sleep.

Characters of a known code:
a fading ever-widened vacuna scar on the arm,
an aging viruela pockmarked face,
the blue threads of varicose-veined legs.

Yes. The body speaks in languages left unread,
and you can only marvel
at the message, literate only in your own.
Awed by stories told by thighs and lips
or the ugliness of the littlest toe.

DECOLONIZING THE MIND

First expiate all sin, erase the Lenten penance and the absolutions.
Believe all miracles are fact; accept all facts as miracles, then
expunge both fact and miracle.

The needle plunges into skin and pst, pst, pst, the germs—the bad
ones—die. Good invisible one, exterminator, how do you explain
success? Cancerous tumors, leukemia erased, deleted, from the body
template? Miracle? These are facts—the cells rebel and immunity
no longer applies. The mind sags with the weight of wars, of battles
lost and won, and finally loses. This game knows no winners.

Then erase allegiance to all flags and feel no goose bumps at parades.
Shed no tears for soldiers, dead or live. See the tricolor and do not
flinch; the redwhiteandblue must leave you free to marvel at the
symmetry of stars. Shed not a tear, sing without quavering voice, or
better still, sing a silent song.

The tongue is next. Speak only life truths in a language yours alone.
Delete "mande" as involuntary response to your name. Make your
name your own, neither Catholic saint nor telenovela fad. Let
words come as they must and as a neurosurgeon might precision
cut the words that oppress, that control, words bad and good that
enslave and hinder, manacles of the colonized mind.

Then, let decolonizing mist into the brain cells where blood knows
no allegiance except its own capillaries. Betrayal by memory banks
closed forever.

And finally, believe that all is not—and that nothing is—like the
yellow explosion of forsythia.

PURPLE FUGUE

Deep blue bruises on fresh wounds,
darker ojeras under eyes vermillion sad,
violet nail polish on sculptured nails
fringe peaceful pianist hands.

You hold your innocence, a fruit not yet ripe,
and your pain is the face of a newborn weeping
without tears, darkened redpurple.
You fear for your girlchild.
The mark darkens on her forehead
bluish veins of blood under bronze brown skin.
¡Pura india!

On the lace-tableclothed tabletop,
grapes from Chile nestle quietly
in grandma's white ceramic bowl.

The past awaits,
tints the day dark and deep.
Outside, figs turn pulpy against
fig-green leaves;
eggplants, organically grown, wait patiently.
Magenta bougainvilleas sing sevillanas at noon,
at sunsets yelling passion and desire;
Teresitas dancing in the morning light,
forget-me-nots, pensamientos, en el viento,
the variegated sheen of a pigeon's soft down,
the quiet constant punzada of internal pain
pulsing pulsing pulsing.

Let's leap into the vortex—
we, the discovery to be made,
the territory to be explored,
a hue hiding at the center,
the color of hope. My passionflower,
expect explosions.

A LOVE POEM, ALAS

For Elvia

A tear trickles down my heart
to the pit   of my insides
where hollowness as vast   as Texas and Arizona combined
opens a Magritte painting to the sky in the eye

You are
an inkling in that unchartered sense that
tells me things—whispers crossword puzzle words,
tells me to turn when you look my way;

You are
secure shore to the tumultuous seas
of my migrant soul
that frames the end of land and sea;

You are
the purity of a smile
and an elevator door closing slowly swiftly
to our locked hearts.

Goose bumps from hair
to toenail, reacting to your voice
calling my name like a mantra.

I search and find you in
full moons
sunsets
a white Persian cat.

An aria hangs in the air
    as the last leaf flutters earthwise
The sound of snow deafens the bright sun and
    the dusky colors of winter
The quiet roar of the fire clings
    to the soft purring of the cat . . . or your snoring.

Silences full of you.

I have stopped reading while I eat (at least when you're around)
have given up chocolate snacks
    and yogurt dinners, and Jeopardy every night,
the peace of my aloneness in the night,
and the fruits of incessant journal entries;

Instead I have a ready ear on mornings
    brimming with dreams just lived
I have gained a touch of eternity,
have acquired a look some call radiant.

I have, I am
You have, you are
Mi otro yo.

LOVERS

Come, I summon you,
ex-lovers who hover
over me in Nepantla.
Reminisce with me,
some nights it's Castilian Spanish brushing my earlobe
whispering Machado or Neruda
humming "una furtiva lagrima . . ."
the sofrito an aftertaste, the smell of Cuban cigars strong as blood.

Other nights, it's a Tejano laugh like rain on the tin roof,
an inviting twinkle in a mejicano eye,
lizard eyes, fixed and deep,
a red chuco bandana and Rubén Naranjo acordeón,
"prisionero de esta cárcel," "¡sí señor!"
the smell of tierra mojada al anochecer,
te de romero, so you'll never forget me,
shared showers embracing me through the night—in lak'ech!

Or it may be Willie con sus "blue eyes crying" que me cubren
con el olor a tequila in a Chicago blues bar in Nebraska,
Mexican dances in Grand Prairie or the Radisson en Lincoln,
donde la raza moves synchronized round and round.
I swirl in Anglo arms confused—cowboy boots by my bed—
long blonde hair in a ponytail,
a child's smile over Custer's moustache,
a new-moon Midwest whiteness,
discussing Bertolucci under the Milky Way.

Women's arms, comforting and sinewy,
spreading wide like wings,
protecting, helping me fly.

STILL TO COME

What I have yet to know intrigues me.
I peer into Tarot—the Priestess, the Hanged Man,
lower arcana, too—
and Spanish playing cards—Bastos, Reina de Espadas.
I search the unknown,
what is still to come,
what I know awaits.

The silence of fireworks in Valencia.
Paella for two through the loneliness of solo dining.
I walk alone on a distant beach—the Mediterranean, the Gulf, the
    Pacific, the Cantabric.
I never fail to find shells, starfish, sand dollars—
omens. Tokens of what is to come.

Dancing Tejano under a Texas sun, innocent as periwinkles.
Danzón in Veracruz, smooth and close as music to gardenias.
Polkas in Monterrey to the accordion's plaintive wail.
In Barcelona the music has its own choreography.

What dance is still to come?
Or is this all there is, my friend,
until the end when nothing is?

MIGRAINE

Talking mouths spew lights into infinity
like sparklers on the Fourth of July
and with black-hole acuity warn of your approach.

I ignore it all, and with the force
of machete blows at 60 mph you arrive:
forehead, temples, neck, my very being
smashed with waves of pain,
overwhelming the calm ridges
of my brain.

I lie in darkness
within the proverbial pit from pole to pole.
Light is searing pain.

You win.

THE BODY/MY BODY

"You can never be thin enough," they said,
but I knew better,
taunted and teased.
Esqueleto rumbero, the kids would tease,
and hot tears would roll down my cheeks;
palillo, and pinche flaquinche—they'd hurl the words.
Flaca, a boyfriend's term of endearment.
But TV cartoons had Olive Oyl,
and Mexican cinema had La Vitola.
Then Twiggy was in and skinny legs.

I had it no easier than Gorda or Tonina Jackson or Toro—
all my friends who plump and happy would beat up on boys
and girls who called them names
and then cry inside,
for sticks and stones may hurt,
but words wound deep and leave scars on the soul.
And now they diet—
some die on the surgeon's table:
liposuction, a nip and a tuck.

Our mothers wore girdles,
now it's Spanx or shapers.
Bulimia or anorexia.
The body is perfection
waiting to be.

Your body is
perfection.

CAPRICHO

Este capricho
ya no lo aguanto
lo llevaré al río
and I'll send it on its way
wish it better luck next time.
No, ya no me aguanto
te devoraré and
spitting out dry bones
useless parts that won't
can't feed my hungers
I'll feel free to
and free from.

Este capricho
se ha anidado en mí
como el vivir de cada día
so subtle I mistook it for love.

¡Pero no! It's capricho,
nothing else
de película
de esos que no duran
que se esfuman al amanecer
después de una noche quesque de amor.

Así, que ya sabes, vete con el sol
a otro mundo raro, donde no haya caprichos.

Vete a volar la huila.
Vete a contarle las muelas a otra.
Vete así como llegaste. Without an invitation.

LAS HIJAS DE JUÁREZ

The brown bodies. The women's brown bodies. Lie in the desert, nestled in the warm desert sand. Earth calling her daughters home. As if they can hear, an ear pressed to the ground.

The women's brown bodies. Brown faces. Lifeless bodies cradle lifeless dreams and desires. Nothing matters—brown bodies no longer feel the cactus thorns piercing skin or the pebbles crushing against a cheek, an arm. These things no longer matter to the brown bodies. The women's brown bodies.

La Llorona roams the dry creek bed wailing for her disappeared daughters. Their brown bodies lifeless. Mutilated. Burnt. Dismembered. Rendered unrecognizable.

Pink crosses sprout on street corners. Faces stare back from flyers. Have you seen . . . ? Hung on the wall, the infamous wall.

The search party finds a shoe in the desert sand, a simple black patent shoe. A hawk flies overhead. Urracas.

Grackles' searing cries seems to call their names—
María.
   Andrea.
        Sofía.
Hundreds more.
   Azucena.
        Sylvia.
            Mercedes.
Las hijas de Juárez.

III

IN THE COUNTRY OF ART

IN THE COUNTRY OF ART

For Amalia Mesa-Bains

Compañera, en tu arte y en tu ser
your topography shapes our world
your life and study.

Heredera de Sor Juana, de las Amazonas y de las Adelitas
surges a la vida making meaning from scratch
from everyday uses and everyday claims;
your nutrient sources son tu vida y las nuestras
your domesticana atraviesa tiempos y espacios,
mother of the land of the dead,
queen of the waters,
reina de lo visible e invisible,
ama y dueña de la vida y la muerte.
There is nothing beyond consideration.
Con Dolores del Río y tus herramientas,
you excavate gendered histories de nosotras, las mujeres.

Your metamemories are mine
and hers
and ours
sigues siendo mujer
sigues siendo fuerza
y sigues siendo luz.

In your country,
art rules y las mujeres son.

ASTUCIA

A SANTA ELENA

Con que astucia
me enredaste in your enmarañada vida
y tu leyenda me sigue desde España
y los judíos, los gitanos,
las gentes de bien y de mal,
hasta Laredo y matachines
danzando a la cruz vestida de flores,
the true cross you
found. You wouldn't let anyone
fool you.

You knew the truth!
Ay, Elena, ¡qué astucia la tuya!
Llegaste hasta este mi pueblo
de tardes de mayo,
soleadas con lloviznas inesperadas,
en día de fiesta de la Santa Cruz,
en Laredo al barrio de la Ladrillera.
La tambora beats out a call
and my heart answers.

CUNNING[§]

TO SANTA ELENA

Cunningly you embroiled me
in your tangled life.
Your legend follows me from Spain.
The Jews and the Gypsies,
those of good and evil.

You follow me to Laredo and the matachines
dancing to a cross bedecked with flowers,
la cruz verdadera que tú
encontraste a tu manera.
No te dejaste engañar.

¡Tú sabias la verdad!
Ay Elena, such cleverness!
You arrived at this my town
of sunny afternoons with unexpected rain showers
on the Day of the Holy Cross
in Laredo al barrio de la Ladrillera.
The drum me llama
y el corazón responde.

---

§   Translated by the author.

A BREATH. A SIGH. A PASSING.

For Gwendolyn Brooks

You say farewell.
As the century ends,
your voice lies silent in our hearts, a breath, a sigh.

Your name sings a song of Chicago over generations,
Gwendolyn Brooks.
Your voice rings in my memory's ear loud,
quietly sure and insistent,
strong as the wind blustery that December afternoon.
Chicago and the MLA—I sit on the floor with others.
We have come to hear you to see you to honor you.
Words dance on the page,
"we be cool" and sit and smile.

In the story,
Maud brings a gift,
a knot at my throat.
So many poem words connecting our souls
I hear the wind whispering city secrets I keep in my heart.
I see the wind, flags whipping lashing out on the flagpole.
I smell the wind full of city smells—gasoline and gardenias—
and feel Chicago in my veins rushing
to the sounds of opera and Jimmy Buffett.
In my soul of souls, you tie it all together with words.

You are gone and we remain
in awe,
celebrating your life,

your spirit.
Blessed by your life.
Amongst the spirits of light, you dwell.
I invoke your name and know your strength,
Gwendolyn Brooks!

SALVAVIDAS

For Adrienne Rich

Life fades into black
The evening sounds
Deafening—
Shrieking, flapping, the grackles claim their roosting spot
And I marvel at their tenacity.
I flash back to a summer
Evening in Nebraska
You laughed quietly at the antics
Of a nervous graduate student
Preening and showing off for you
I sat on the sidelines
Ever the observer, the witness
And you came over and reached across my shyness
Throwing a life raft
And I was saved.

A SOR JUANA

Juana. Inés, ¿cómo es que aguantaste tanto?
How did you survive? Or did you?
I feel your heavy habit on my thin shoulders,
on my legs, rough spun stockings,
the chin pinched tight as an orange—de esas de Sevilla—
and your words,
your daring words,
circumscribe your world,
expand it.

Your world popped into mine,
y me enseñaste:
    fearlessly you faced
    them all—your critics,
            your family,
            your lovers,
            your teachers,
            detractors and supporters,
            men and women
who didn't
understand,
    didn't know
            you.

I was lost in a book; you saved me.
    You found me
            in an imaginable future
                    a mere flicker in your time and space.

You rescued me from the abyss,
    from a life   without poetry,
                       without prayer,
                       without women.

You are the savior
    the longed for
            the dreamed for—
                        feared yet welcomed.

It was 1970, and your collected works,
    a gift for my twenty-third birthday,
saved me
    from myself.
            ¡Gracias!

WINTER BIRDS

The gaggle of geese fly in formation
    across the slate gray skies,
        smoothly glide, then land on the ice.
Omens? Signifiers? Of what?
Portents of grace? Simulacrum for thoughts
    by nature, hobbled together into symmetry.
    The water, frozen in wintry splendor
        beneath them, courses on its way
        to ice.

Wild turkeys have come, too.
    They land all in a row, forage
        with claw and beak,
          find little food
          remain steadfast in their search.

The cardinals sporting winter coats
    flitter through the bushes;
        the flecks of feathers on their crop
          flutter in the wind.
Eyes shimmer above orangy beaks.
At least three females, maybe five,
    find refuge scaling the icy
        wintry wind and ice.

A red flash flits across, and
    off they go to the leafless
        maple. Perched above

they cock their heads as if
    tuning in through static,
    finding the right frequency.
Their message strong:
    survival above all else.

And I marvel at all their shapes,
    their survival—
they are frocked in tranquil pursuit,
    in midflight effortlessly
        stooping to look for food.
A morsel, a seed, a crumb,
perhaps a lone worm still there under
    the elm's leaves golden brown
    like honey or molasses. Or both.
I rejoice in their tenacity,
their survival.
I remain a winter bird
surviving in alien lands.

SEASONED TRAVELER

The seasons startle me
with their simplicity.
    I arrive in midwinter
            to snowdrifts and sleet.
    Beware of black ice, everyone warns.
I learn to wear layers, snow boots, and wool scarves,
to find comfort in the white blanket,
    the quiet melting.
            Learn to be still.

Spring arrives with the yellow of forsythia.
The robin's song and the tulip facing the sun
find me marveling at the miracle—
snow melts, bulbs sprout, squirrels frolic,
climb the magnolia's limbs.

Soon summer peeks through
    a sliver of warmth but quickly retreats
            as the last snow falls in May.
Too soon the sweltering heat,
    the harsh sun and the long days of summer
            porch evenings. The warming lays out a picnic blanket.
I wear sandals again, toes liberated at last!

Then fall arrives with glorious golden splendor.
    Pumpkins grace front yards;
    pumpkin soup and pumpkin bread.
Bright shiny faces at our door: trick or treat!

The squirrels make quick use of the acorns.
Honey colored leaves carpet, soften the gentle crunch underfoot.

Too soon, winter comes. The icy morning
    shimmers along the path, along the edge of
        reality.

I brace myself: don scarf, layers, boots,
as in a dream I bundle up, sip hot soup,
   and wander through golden magic
       in the early darkening of day to night.
The ever-present cycle, quotidian and familiar,
living a day at a time; the ever-spinning earth
around the sun must follow its destiny
as I do mine, a seasoned traveler at last.

SUCCUMB TO WEATHER

The weather map on TV like
A children's school assignment:
Each state, lined in black, the blustery
Snowfall, the sleet and hail, all
Decked out in pinks and blues. Shades of green and yellow

My life, a weather map
Under clouds of color with highs and lows,
Arrows indicating direction
Crisscrossing my being.
The heart under a gray cloud.
Snow predicted for three o'clock—
In time for the afternoon commute.
It will be messy out there!

KANSAS CITY SHIFT

Spring comes suddenly—
one morning, the daffodils bloom and
defy the snow-covered ground
with their impetuous yellow. Then the forsythia.
Next come the crocuses, and finally the roses,
each taking turns astonishing.

I am mute, quietly melt like the snow and ice,
my heart singing the morning birdsong
of my being. Jubilant. Alive.

How is it that the snow hums as it melts?
How is it that the clouds make way to sunny days?
And the robin's egg blue?

How is it that amidst such transformation,
life seeps forward—or backward?
Throwback Thursday on Facebook and
pictures of our before selves greet and
force memories shoehorned into today.

Like weather, life shifts.
Children die—drive-bys.
Governments starve citizens.
Down the street a body lies.
Brown bodies die crossing a river.
Black bodies die crossing a street.
We all die a little each time a leaf falls
each time a heart stops beating.

POETRY AND WINE

For Tom and Whitney

The poet sat back and almost fell
as our broken chair startled: two seconds, maybe one.
As in a movie, the red red wine spilt onto
the white white tablecloth turned black
as the darkening evening stained the blue sky.
Embarrassment and awe and apology and poetry
snuck in the back door.
The party was over; and the white tablecloth had survived,
had been spared accidental merlot spills.
But destiny brought the poet to our front door, to our table.
And the chair creaked, and the back gave, and his glass tipped.
Just like life: in a second what was thought safe
was not.

INSOMNIA IN MADRID

For Meg Greer

five a.m.
sleepless night behind me
looking out the window
one of many windows
looking for another living soul
like Beckett's Nana
finding
window after window
after window darkened—
blinds drawn—
finally finding comfort
in a light
a single philistine light
finds me smiling with a thought
the thought of
another living soul
a single other living soul
smoking a cigarette sitting
by a window
one of many windows
waiting for the sunrise
for arising
waiting for another also rising sun
waiting for a reason
for a reason for living
for a reason for sleeping
waiting
by a window
one of many windows
waiting

IV

MIEL DE MESQUITE

MIEL DE MESQUITE

Every spring,
explosion of new green
surprises me.
The mesquite in our yard wears an Easter frock,
accessorized with yellow blossoms.
Soon, the fruit, juicy and crunchy at once,
will weigh down scrawny limbs.
De niña,
on lazy dusky evenings,
after homework,
after playing a las escondidas,
I harvested bean pods,
la miel from the tree trunk.
I chewed on sweet mesquite fruit.
We—siblings and neighbors—
trade stories in the dimming eve
as we go through pod after pod.
The waxing moon can't wait to be full.
Soon Mami calls our names:
Norma, Tino, Laura, Elsa, Lety . . .
Mari, Sandra, Celia, Julio . . .
Geri, Ricky!
In her eighties alone, Mami dwells in the past:
where children still
crowd around for dinner—bean tacos
and cinnamon tea with milk.
Ghost children—
laughing, playing, arguing, crying, sleeping—

keep her company.
The mesquite still there. Still surprises me.
La miel de mesquite
still sweet
still lingers.

EL DÍA DE LA CONEJA

Antes sí, throngs would visit seven churches—the holy images:
    Virgins, saints, crosses all covered with purple cloth—every Holy
    Thursday después de que el padrecito would wash the feet of twelve
    monaguillos (or members of the Altar Society). You had to be
    male—after all, Christ didn't bother washing the feet of women.

The churches filled with prayer: Vía Crucis every Friday of Lent, and
    on Good Friday las siete palabras at 3 p.m., holy water, el Sábado
    de Gloria. Easter Sunday's resurrection heralded by choirs rejoicing,
    and everyone wears something new. Mami sewing late on Saturday
    night so her children can estrenar Easter outfits.

Lenten foods every Friday and Holy Week: albóndigas de camarón,
    powdered shrimp in egg batter light and fluffy. Enchiladas de queso
    blanco and fish sticks cuando no hay dinero for real fish. Nopalitos
    from the nopalera at the ranch where you can cut your own or from
    Doña María, who sells them peeled and sliced and ready to cook.
    For dessert, capirotada: cheese and nuts and raisins and the syrup
    made with anise tea and piloncillo layered on day-old french bread.

The rosary every night at home kneeling around Papi praying—the
    monotony of each Hail Mary, each Our Father, the litanies to Our
    Lady, metaphors defying the imagination: torre de marfil, vaso de
    justicia, rosa mística. And Mami reciting the final prayers—"Por
    estos misterios santos de que hemos hecho recuerdo, te pedimos, O
    María . . ."

Easter crowds of yesterday prayed, wept for el Cristo inerte en la igle-
    sia Santo Niño en Nuevo Laredo. Another in San Agustin Church
    in Laredo.

En la frontera, Easter arrives each year amid the hustle and bustle
     of Semana Santa shoppers from Mexico. License plates: Jalisco.
     Michoacán, Jalapa. Estado de México. Long lines to cross the river,
     the long lines at Walmart. Long lines at the mall.

Spring breakers from Houston and Dallas crowd the shops en el mer-
     cado, sipping margaritas and buying trinkets.

Men wearing Mexican hats declare bottles of Cuervo and Kahlúa, go
     home to Houston, Dallas, or Wisconsin. Women buy jewelry, shop
     for bargains, weep to see the children begging. A three-year-old
     selling Chiclets will haunt their nightmares.

Finally, the fasting over, the privations ended, we chew gum again, go
     to the movies, eat chocolate, play jacks, jump rope, wear lipstick—
     be free to be!

La Coneja leaves Easter baskets full of confetti-filled cascarones and
     too much candy—marshmallow peeps, bunnies, and eggs que
     empalagan. She brings bunny shaped piñatas to break at the ranch,
     or at least the roadside rest stop where we eat our picnic lunch or
     cook carne asada with the requisite potato salad and sopa de arroz.

At Lake Casa Blanca or Chavana's Ranch the music blares, accordion
     and bajo sexto under skies so blue it hurts as much as the flour-
     filled cascarón a cousin breaks on a favorite aunt's head.

Easter Monday everything goes back to normal. Only memories
     fading with age.

Easters away from the border find me yearning for all of it: foods,
     prayers, incense, the unending faith of a people rich in tradition
     and longing. Resurrection and redemption bleed through the mes-
     sage of salvation. It's Easter after all.

FIESTAS DE DICIEMBRE

How can I ignore the season's celebratory air
when my neighbor's yard has sprung a plastic life-size nacimiento
since mid-November?
On every bush and tree, tiny lights flicker like colored fireflies,
in syncopated rhythm, and here and there luminarias light the way.

At the mall and downtown, shoppers rush and bustle
like bees around a hive;
"Jingle Bells" and carols a la country or Tejano
mixed in with Bing Crosby and Dolly Parton
flood the airwaves.
Even the Mexico City station plays "I'm Dreaming of a White
    Christmas."

It begins with the first novena a la virgen,
the procession, the all-night vigil, matachines dancing
and the mariachis singing las "Mañanitas Guadalupanas"
at dawn on her day.
In Mexico City, in D.C., in Tokyo, danzantes gather
to honor the Goddess of Tepeyac,
she of the starry manto with a moon at her feet.
On my altar, a candle defies the darkness and wins.

Then las posadas
con sus rituals of begging
"E-e-n nombre del cie-elo . . ."
and yes, partying;
a holy night reenacted in the barrio streets—
from Cantarranas to El Chacón

the procession proceeds por calles polvorientas
in the quiet of evening—
en el crepúsculo between day and night.

In Mexico City, crowds attend pre-posadas and pastorelas
from Marxist nineteenth-century texts full of capitalist devils
and Vatican hermits; while Bato and Gila,
eternal Acadian shepherds,
instruct with simple theology.

At the corner, en el barrio Las Cruces,
on brisk evenings, los pachucos
light a small fire, tell lies and brag
of Christmases past. El relaje alive and well;
hearts beating under tatooed skin,
survivors of life's wars, and Korea, Vietnam.

When Nochebuena finally comes,
grateful families gather, enjoy the season's
pozole, tamales con café o champurrado
(even on warm December nights),
cinammony sweet buñuelos
and ojarascas o pan de polvo o bizcochitos.

Yet others sleep away the hunger, the pain,
toss and turn under thin sheets made from flour sacks,
dream of Santa Claus, los Reyes Magos, toys, food,
and no one shouting,
no one fighting,
no one cussing,
no one searing the night's air
with thin wailing.

Lucky children break piñatas,
celebrate con colaciones and

firecrackers—sparklers: ephemeral light shows spinning
in the dark.

A star glistens in the velvet sky
and Laredo welcomes the Christ child with
gunshots and cuetes,
the smell of powder mixed with carne asada.

En la Misa de Gallo,
estrenando Christmas finery,
those who can, celebrate.
Those who don't lie forgotten,
forgetting in their sleep.

Distant stars know nothing of earth's
rejoicing or of earth's eternal spin on a silent axis.

LA LLORONA CONSIDERS THE STATE OF TORTILLAS

She knows they sell them in neat packages
Cellophaned and counted.

They come in whole wheat, yellow, or white corn,
Even red tinted and crisp, ready for tostadas or chalupas
Too easy it seems to her for the truth to be told

She also knows machines can never render
A product true

If flour . . . one misses
The familiar smell of dough cooking on the comal
The puffing up one must, simply must, pat down
To hear the pooof of air escaping
The taste—hot off the comal, melting butter or honey

If corn,
The smell is sweeter
The touch rougher
The taste has vestiges of corn on the cob
Or pinole . . . él que tiene más saliva traga más pinole
Weeping woman weeps to see
That chemicals preserve and make these tortillas last

I could write poems on the smooth surface
Or fold them up and eat them
Tortillas are
At once food and utensil

I scoop up memories with each bite,
And La Llorona

Weeping woman smiles.

BULLFIGHT

I am the bull dragged
across a sandy bullring in Cancún,
a carcass, spent and bled to death.

The tourists—Japanese, German, Chicano, and even gringos—
don't know they just witnessed a travesty, they cheer
a gutted ritual. No honor. No glory.

I gave my life for this?
When I was poked and raced into the ring,
I moved just so,
escaped the ribbon marker.
"Saltillero" me nombraron,
a worthy name, an honorable name.

Puny men tease me,
poke and try to anger me.
They fail.
The banderillero, big as a bull,
rides a horse, poor beast of burden;
pokes and fails.

The sharp knife enters swiftly,
and I know what's coming. Feel it
as sure as I breathe,
with nostrils wide, huffing.

I see dark pink—the matador's cape,
    shiny sequins in black and white.
I am color-blind, you say.

So I've heard, but I assure you I hear the color,
smell the red of blood and the brown of sun-bronzed skin.

Movement I must follow;
perplexed and tired, I sniff the earth,
following my scent
to the source of death.

He bends, and I hear, "Olé."
I flick an ear,
the right, then the left;
I flick my tail.
I stand calmly,
appear not interested,
then I follow through
to my imminent end.

The crowd roars and stands;
I lie and die
on a Wednesday afternoon
en Cancún.
Red with beer and sun,
the tourists cheer
amid the stench of blood and sweat.

It's five o'clock
on a Wednesday in Cancún.
I die.

PLATICANDO CON MANUELA

Para Manuela Solís Sager

Manuelita, Mela. Manuela. Miss Solís. Mrs. Sager.
¿Cuál de todas eres tú?
All of them, of course.

At my kitchen table, we sit and sip
manzanilla tea. Platicando,
an ocean of memories come flooding
of your life en Las Minas when you were
a young Gila en la pastorela,
wearing a plain white dress and the red hato your mother made.

Memories as vivid as the bluebonnets in the fields in spring
and the twinkling of the fireflies in the darkening dusk.
Elementary school en Laredo and a joyous childhood.
La familia at the center of it all.
You tell of being a young teen off to learn the ways of the world.
The party paid for the train ticket,
but you had to refashion donated dresses,
buy new shoes for the journey.

And your father fearing for you yet proud.
The twinkle in his eye told you more than his
mumbled blessing,
"Vaya con Dios, m'ija,"
while your mother stifled sobs caught in her throat
and hugged and kissed you at home.
Couldn't go to the station to see you off. Too painful.
Too public a display of love.
Your thin arms, your strong body. Your sharp eye and mind
ready to handle anything.

And because you loved hats, and gloves,
y era la moda,
you go on your way wearing a gray suit,
matching gloves and hat.
The hatpin belonged to your tía
and that first pair of pumps pinched your feet.
You brace yourself, tighten your grip
on the small brown suitcase and go, head high,
to conquer the world alongside
Emma and Carmen and Luisa and so many other women.
And men, you would remind me. They too were there, fighting
with us. Striking and marching. Fighting for justice. It was the hard
times, the dark times of rinches and sheriffs and judges
who kept Mexicans in their place.

Through the hard times. And the good.
The strikes and the sit-ins. The pecan shellers.
The mills. A living wage. Safe working conditions.
Not too much to ask, is it?

You marry, y la familia has much to say:
some are happy, others not.
He's not one of us.
But love conquers all. Or so you have been told.
Jim is proud. You make a life.
When your son is born you rejoice in him.

You never gave up, did you, Manuela?
Marching for the ERA, protesting with the farmworkers,
leading boycotts and marches and sit-ins.
Always there for the women: Primavera en Laredo,
for women's history en San Antonio,
supporting artists, your politics out there—strong and firm.
You prevailed, you survived. You taught by example
that one's life matters. That one person CAN make a difference.
¡Gracias, Manuela!

FORJANDO EL DESTINO

For Emma Tenayuca

In the photo you are a young, impassioned speaker,
fist raised. I can hear your voice, loud and clear.
I ask, "What gave you the courage, Emma?"
I know the answer.
With youth's passion you fought injustice
fought for pecan shellers—women, young and old, and children too.

You worked alongside them
and smelled the acrid smell
and felt the stifling heat
and the dust covered your hands and your hair
in spite of the scarf you wore
and you heard them cough
and you laughed with them
and you cried with them
until it was time to say no more
no more to wage cuts
no more to unsafe conditions.

Time for the struggle to begin.
Time for destiny to carry you on its wings.
You had a gift. And you used it.
Others followed. Twelve thousand workers walked away
from poorly paid jobs
and the bosses had to listen
and the papers had to cover the story
and you won. And lost.
Had to go on your way.

Destiny led you to California, away from the ex-husband,
away from the embarrassed relatives,
the nosy neighbors,
the prying reporters.
And destiny brought you back
a teacher,
a shaper of young minds,
to sustain language and culture,
fighting injustice in another terrain.
Your razor-sharp mind never at rest, always working,
always thinking. The words and the thoughts almost
too much. The books, the papers, your work.

Honor and glory came late;
your memory lives in the hearts of those who knew you,
those who never met you but honor your passion
and join you in the struggle still not won.

¡Adelante!

OF MATH, WORDS, AND MRS. WATKINS

Red peonies on her desk and the smell of Dial soap
so strong it makes me sneeze,
in her algebra class I daydream
to the drone of her crackly old-woman's voice.

Ninth-grade algebra was my best subject;
there were only finite answers,
clear, crisp.
As predictable as sunlight
theorems always always answered the question.
The problems all had solutions,
but I didn't convince Mrs. Watkins
that my destiny lay in math.

No, she believed I would end up a statistic
of a different sort. An unwed mother or at best a working girl—
an office clerk for Central Power and Light Company,
a sales clerk at J. C. Penney.

"Those are dreams," she says
when I share with her my dream of becoming a physicist.
And she was right,
I had dreams.
Join the school paper staff, she advised,
not the slide rule team;
she trusted my love of words,
didn't see my love of numbers.
And thus my path was set.

The precision of a destiny shaped
by a few words let loose, strewn about
without thought,
like startled pigeons flying into the sky.
"Those are dreams," she said, and I believed her
and stopped dreaming about numbers and settled
to a life of words and dreams of a different sort.
No. I didn't become a physicist, but for seven years
I was an office clerk at Central Power and Light Company.

A poet clicking away at the manual typewriter
where the clicking rhythm spewed ugly words
and good ones, too. But mostly it was the numbers.
I relished memorizing numbers: addresses, account numbers,
meter readings, and the formulas for fuel adjustments.
Yes, math served me well at CP&L,
but it was too late. I had caught the other bug,
and words would not let me be. Words.
Mrs. Watkins knew it all along.

RAILROAD WORKER

My grandfather Maurilio laid railroad tracks,
did whatever the company asked.
His strong brown body working day in and day out
in Corpus, in San Antonio in the yards.
Tejano and proud, he'd smoke his hand-rolled Buglers.
Played his guitar singing his own songs.

The railroad ruled.
He and Celia and their children ate
and slept and partied according to the yard's schedule.
The thinking, too, was circumscribed by rails
and whistles blowing as loud as the hopes and dreams
of moving on.

The railroad in Texas hired Mexicans:
Tex-Mex. Union Pacific. Southern Pacific.
'Buelito wore his blue striped cap and union overalls.
Each morning, took his blue—or was it black?—enameled
lunch box, portavianda he called the three neatly stacked pots,
and in the afternoon, took it home and set it up on the cupboard,
el trastero he made with his own hands.
The railroad took his best years.

Between sixteen and forty, he worked every day.
Until one day he left. A promised promotion
went to a white man instead. He argued in vain
with the white bosses who
had always treated him well,

made him trust them with their smiles and
their praises for his work.

He left. Or they fired him.
The story is never really clear. He was a union man.
In the end, it doesn't matter. The family was deported to Mexico.

It was the 1930s, and the law allowed it:
The deportation of mejicanos like Maurilio and Celia
and their Texas-born daughters.
His faith destroyed, his hurt so deep, he never recovered.
Drank his life away,
a railroad worker without a railroad to work.

¡ÓRALE!

A RETIREMENT POEM

For Romeo Rodríguez on the occasion of his retirement

Life meets us along our path with
one undeniable brutal truth
clashing against our reality—change.

Hoy día, our friend, our colleague,
Romeo, takes one more step along
the path we all must follow, haciendo
camino al andar por senderos
not always known, not always welcomed
but, yes, always offering life lessons.

A life shaped by hard work,
blessed with a family—at home and at work;
una vida colmada with the trials and joys of living.
Seeing infants become children become teens become adults,
we see our own mortality in our everyday joys.

Una taza de café,
cenzontles singing in the early morning,
the purring of the car's newly tuned engine,
a good day at work,
a good talk with coworkers, with friends,
at the end feeling satisfied with what's been done,
offering sincere thanks for a day well lived.

And at retirement,
life takes a different turn,
blessings manifold.

Take stock, Romeo, and feel proud,
you have built this school, too,
contributed to the education of those who come
to fulfill dreams.
You have offered tu granito de arena
and with a smile, a good morning, a handshake,
you have shown us lo que es ser buen educado,
what it means to be a real person, a civil human being,
hombre de palabra.
Gracias. Gracias for the lessons.
Thank you for the ready helping hand,
the sincere best wishes, the energy of your labor.
Gracias y buena suerte.

EL MEJICANO Y LA CHICANA

He was from over there, a mexicano, and she was from over here
del otro lado, a chicana.
They met en una discoteca in Nuevo Laredo
on a Saturday night when the place was really hot
and humid and the music loud and sexy.
They danced. He kissed her. That was it. They never dreamed
that ten years later, they would end up at the same—
the very same—office working side by side
en una agencia aduanal.
He did the paper work for his side, and she, for hers.
They remembered
the dance. The kiss.
And so it happened that they left their spouses.
They lived together for a while, and a few years later,
they married. They had two girls and two boys.
And they lived happily ever after.
At least so the story goes . . .
but no one can give me their names!

SYLVIA, PATO, AND THE HIPPIE

He rode his motorcycle to the border
from the East Coast, Maine or Vermont, quien sabe.
It was the '60s and he wanted adventure.
Long blonde hair in a ponytail,
Sylvia was a nurse at Mercy Hospital,
engaged to Humberto, aka Pato.

The crash was a silly mishap. He ended up in the hospital.
Nothing too serious—a broken leg and broken rib.
It was the earring, she claimed, that
made her fall in love.
From one day to the next it seemed
they fell in love and married—
a big wedding at San Agustin Church.
    Next door to where Sylvia had gone to high school.
With time came disagreements, cultural adjustments.
Minor problems and a few serious bumps along the road.
But they weathered them.
They just celebrated fifty years of marriage.
Three children—all grown now.

Pato got married, too.
He went back to his high-school sweetheart
who had been waiting for him to get over Sylvia—
took three years. In another three, she died of breast cancer.
Pato waited but now has a boyfriend, a gringo from up north.
Así es la vida, uno propone y Dios dispone.

LOS CARTONEROS

I

Los cartoneros work and work at a job unlike any other.
They scour the city on their bicycles built for cartoneando,
a welded rack, a crate, a three-by-three-foot space
before them.
They gather cardboard,
discarded refuse from downtown businesses.
Janitors know them well, have their favorites;
for them, they flatten boxes,
stack them out on the sidewalk where
pedestrians hustle by on their way al otro lado,
some going, some coming
to Mexico,
to the United States.
And the cardboard treasure will bring a
living wage, depending on the living.

But sometimes they find other treasures.
Those less secure, the new ones, venture out and scour neighborhoods
scavenging what others discard
and their reward—that which no longer works,
which lies broken, which is obsolete,
a TV, an old chair, a broken vase, a doll,
plastic flowers faded reds and blues,
and they cart it all across to sell, to resell, to recycle.

II

Don Pedrito knows the game,
has the timing just right to get the best loads.
But his broken heart feels flat as the cardboard.
He cries into his beard
as his rough brown hands
hold on to the home-fashioned handlebars.
He cringes even now, twenty years later, remembering her words,
    "Me voy, no eres nada. Ya no aguanto más."
She left with the children and the dog. But he went on.
Consolation, even now, is a bottle of tequila from the deposito
near the house he shares with his nephew's family.
His cuartito clean and sparse. Así es la vida.

III

Doña Meche plans and scrapes to build her humble home,
keeping the best—a piece of tin, a mirror, hardly broken—
for herself. Her children in school and helping out
after crying in the night under starry Mexican skies,
ranchera music on a radio in the distance.
"Esta vida mejor que se acabe / No es para mí / Pobre de mí,"
por un amor o por un dolor, o por ser y vivir en la frontera.
She prays, and she crosses herself, exhausted,
aching muscles and feet; she dreams of swimming in the river
when she was a child, carefree.
Fifty years dissolve, the water is clear.
There is a flood, and her parents drown.
She goes to the orphanage, El Sagrado Corazón.
At thirteen she leaves to become a servant.
The man of the house rapes her; she escapes.
Becomes a prostitute en la Zona.
Finds Jesus, and la Virgencita de Guadalupe

helps her out of one hell.
And life goes on. The struggle.
Cartonera, she sells cans and cardboard.
Carton. It's like gold, she says.
She's learned to read the Tarot to make a little extra,
money that she keeps in a tin can for emergencies.

IV

Emilio's young, pero tampoco too young.
Still has dreams. One day. One day he'll leave,
cross the river. Work hard. Earn money. Fall in love—
he'll be free to love there, not like here.
He knew from childhood he was different.
Only ten when his mother died.
Not long after, his father overdosed.
¿Y ahora qué? he asked.
For the next six years he lived with his secret
en casa de su tía. Not a bad life. He worked
selling newspapers, shone shoes, ran errands.
Until his uncle threw him out. Por maricón, he said.
Milo hung out with the cartoneros and others like him,
found a community. But not for long. Soon he'll leave.
Cross the river. Work hard. Earn money. Fall in love.

EN HONOR DE SU CUMPLEAÑOS[1]

CORRIDO PARA LAURA RENDÓN

En un barrio de Laredo, año del '48
nacio linda morenita,
Laura Rendón se llamó,
Laura Rendón se llamó.

Con regalos y con mimas, su gente la bendició.
Y con cariños y pobreza,
la niña Laura creció,
la niña Laura creció.

Trabajó por aquellos rumbos, y miseria conoció.
Fue en el famoso Western Grill
donde Laurita jaló,
donde Laurita jaló.

Aun siendo high schooler La Laura bien trabajó.
Saliendo ya de Laredo,
a Houston se dirigió,
a Houston se dirigió.

Allá por San Antonio, en SAC estudios cursó.
Desde Houston
a Laredo volvió,
a Laredo volvió

¶ To be sung to the tune of "El corrido de Rosita Alvírez."

99

Y chorro de alumnos forjó.
Después se fue a tierras kineñas
donde maestría logró,
donde maestría logró.

Buscando mejores frutos, a lejanas tierras se fue.
Sufriendo fríos
su doctorado sacó,
su doctorado sacó.

Ya en su pueblo de Laredo, con ganas se dedicó.
Jalando en LJC,
a Las Mujeres formó,
a Las Mujeres formó.

En Washington años duró
hasta salir de esa burrocracia y llegar a la universidad.
Muy lejos se fue,
muy lejos se fue.

Paso por las Carolinas y de ahí en Arizona se refugió.
Y al llegar a sus cincuenta
a las Califas se fue,
a las Califas se fue.

Yo ya con esta me despido, pues he llegado
al final de los versos queridos
de la profe Laurita Rendón,
de la profe Laurita Rendón.

Vuela, vuela, linda y blanca palomita
no te vayas a perder. Llévale este corridito
con buenos deseos a mi fiel amiga Laurita,
mi fiel amiga Laurita.

V

GOING HOME

GOING HOME

They tell me I can't go home again
yet I go home each day after the office,
after pizza with girlfriends,
after a movie at the Cineplex,
after out-there things, I come home.

In November in D.C.,
I exit the Metro station to the daily
"Spare your change?" of the homeless man with the blue hat.

At the bus stop,
I wait with the young mother and her sick child coming home from
    the clinic.
I wait with the two giggling teens—eloquent braided hair—coming
    home from middle school.
I wait with the Ethiopian grandmother—wearing a white halo—car-
    rying two sacks full of groceries.
I wait with the Salvadoran woman coming home from cleaning other
    peoples' homes.
I wait with the young black man trying to look nonthreatening.
I wait with the loud, angry black man wearing a black T-shirt—white
    letters proclaim, "O. J. is innocent."
The bus door sighs open, and we clamber on politely, standing at the
    door, not shoving, just pushing ourselves forward.

I sit by the window. Cocooned in the bus we feel safe.
On my right a child repeats over and over, "I ain't scared, I ain't."
And it becomes a mantra—her awareness elsewhere.

We ride in the silent noisy bus making gear sounds and brake sounds,
    and traffic roars outside.
We ride with our sadness, wear our weariness like a cape.
The mother finally snaps,
"Shut up, or I'll smack you."
The child's awareness returns.
Startled, she puts her tiny hands to her ears,
eyes big as the November moon rising in the east.

It's my stop; I walk home in the darkening eve.
The chant continues in my mind—
I ain't scared, I ain't
I ain't scared, I ain't
I ain't scared, I ain't
I ain't.

CANTANDO LLEGO

For the students and poets at Cigarroa Middle School in Laredo, Tejas, who asked
what inspires my poetry

I arrive with a song,
an old song,
a song as old as the beating of a heart,
and you listen, atentos,
con el corazón hambriento,
hungry for your story—tu historia
herstory
history
our story—
la China Poblana, Aztlán, Huitzilopochtli, el Grito de Dolores.

I listen to your poems:
Miguel Hidalgo, la bandera.
Your pride in who you are
se escurre en las palabras,
"Skin the color of sand at the beach."

As I read my poems,
I peer into Aztec eyes,
    Mayan eyes,
              Coahuiltecan eyes.
My soul fills
as I see my words
strike home,
    move minds
          and hearts.
I feel young energy
in your smiles and your tears

that carry me back to 1963,
Lamar Junior High,
and never a mention of 16 de septiembre
or things I knew or loved.

Yes, things have changed.
And on this sixteenth of September,
I honor you and your future:

Juan
Amanda
Viviana
Enrique
Teresa
Michael

I sing a song
to the four winds and
¡viva México!
   ¡viva Laredo!
        ¡viva la Raza!
until you too shall rejoice in your heart.
You too shall sing your truth.
Like Aztec scribes,
you will write the new codex!

OLMEC HEADS

En la frontera, in Laredo,
the sun is setting, gigantic
as an Olmec head. Sitting by a
crackling fire in the soft night,
I think of the perfect geometry of orbs,
the simplicity of a pyramid.

Remember colossal Olmec heads
removed
    relocated
          re-membered,
how they lie silent in museums
   in Xalapa,
         in Santiago Tuxtla,
            in Mexico City.

The heads haunt
my daily life like a tune
I can't quite name,
ever present like my breath,
mysterious as the silence of dusk.
Far away from their Veracruz home,
they abide in me, in my bones.

ON MY ALTAR

La Virgen de Guadalupe
reigns above
    sacred ancient shards that
        share a space with
Raúl's photo in D.C.'s cold January.
    I on my way to Spain,
        he on his AIDS journey
    that will end in San Antonio,
in spring, five years later.

On my altar
    a corn goddess—a skull crowns her—
        holds ears of corn.
            She's full of gifts.
Santa Teresita, bríndame tu paz.
    San Ramón, ponle un tapón.
        San José y San Pancracio
    each helping out—finding a home, finding a job.
Nestled among the photos and the holy cards and the bultos,
    San Judas Tadeo with his fiery crown
        belonged to Juan Antonio, long gone.
And milagritos—an arm, a breast, a book, a car—
    thanksgiving for healing, for goals achieved.

        Each morning and each night,
          I stand
            sit
          kneel
       before my sacred space.

Each photo holds prayers
    suspended on the tiny dust particles,
        ions of memory binding them
  all
      to me.
My altar alive with blood red roses
    y recuerdos.
        For now, all's right with the world.

DESPEDIDAS

At the mere prospect,
my heart becomes
rock.
Stone.
Hard crystal.

Despedidas.
I do them badly
   y muy apenas.
         A rechina dientes
I offer my cheek,
   a hand, a hug, and
         walk away into a plane,
a car,
   a bus,
         a train,
into the night.
   Me voy con el sol.
         Never look back.

Despedidas.
   With a hug and a kiss
   I utter the good-bye words.
   And shudder.

B'bye
   Have a good life
         Hasta la vista

Ciao

Bueno, bye

When he was about to go,
   my father wanted to say good-bye,
       wanted a farewell ritual. "I don't know how to die,"
         he called out.
   But it is his last breath that I remember.
     His despedida.

GREETINGS IN WHITE

Full-moon night.
Not even Midol helps the cramping.
White carnations, white roses, greet
me   as the white Persian
meows a greeting,   a demand for food y sus
quince minutos de caricias
(that we all know cats must have).

The white lace curtains don't,
they don't,
flutter in the artificial air conditioning.
The white lace sighs, and the fern's quiet green listens.

"You have ten messages," the electronic voice proclaims:
and I listen to the six cries for attention
    and four frustrated hang-ups.
The white roses you sent two days ago bleed in the moonlight.
"Where are you?" your voice asks the wind.
"That was your last message."
I press cancel.
"I will cancel your messages."
I sigh, a rose letting go of its petals.
Letting go of your voice.
Letting go of you.

HABLANDO DE LA VIDA
Y LA MUERTE

Cuando hablo de los que yacen muertos
en el río al amanecer
o de los que pierden
    brazos
            piernas
y hasta la vida
por el afán de irse al norte
hablo de todos nosotros
aun los que jamás han pisado esta mi frontera.

Cuando hablo de desaparecidos
los que perseguidos por pensar
    por hablar
            por escribir
                por ser
los que con el miedo acuestas huyen
o no
hablo de todos nosotros
aún todos los que jamás han tenido idea de lo que es militar por un
    ideal.

Cuando hablo de los miles muertos en guerras
los heridos
los exterminados en hornos o en fosos en
My Lai
    Auschwitz
            Hiroshima
                Tamaulipas

hablo de todos nosotros aun los que con historia y con conciencia
niegan su historia y su conciencia.

Cuando hablo de Tlatelolco
Tenochtitlan
   Wounded Knee
        Rwanda
            Acteal
            Juárez

hablo de nosotros, de todos nosotras
y hablo de ayer y hablo de ahora.

SPEAKING OF LIFE AND DEATH

When I speak of those who lie dead
in the river at dawn
or those who lose
    arms
           legs
                    and even life

because of their intense desire to go north
I speak of all of us
even those who have never set foot on my borderlands.

When I speak of the disappeared
those who were persecuted for thinking
for speaking
    for writing
           for being
those who flee with fear on their shoulders
or not
I speak about all of us
even those who have never had an idea
of what it is to fight for a dream.

When I speak of the thousands dead in war
or the wounded
those exterminated in ovens or pits
My Lai,
    Auschwitz,
           Hiroshima,
                Tamaulipas

I speak of all of us
even those who with history and consciousness
deny their history and their conscience.

When I speak of Tlatelolco
    Tenochtitlan
            Wounded Knee
                Rwanda
                    Acteal
                        Juárez
I speak of ourselves of all of us
I speak of yesterday
I speak of today.

FORTY-THREE

Forty-three students vanished
On September 26, 2014.
Students from Raúl Isidro Burgos Rural Teachers' College.
Missing. Forty-three students.
From Ayotzinapa, Guerrero, to
Iguala, Guerrero,
They traveled
Protesting. Holding in their hearts a passion
Blooming against injustice and oppression,
Protesting discriminatory hiring and funding practices,
The Mexican government.

Forty-three.
Forty-three students intercepted
During their journey by local police.
A confrontation ensued.
What happened during and after the clash
Remains unclear.
Six lay dead.
The official investigation concluded
Once the students were in custody.
They were handed over to the local
Guerreros Unidos
Crime syndicate.
Forty-three students
During the journey.
Forty-three.

HOME

I awaken to the sound of a rooster crowing,
the smell of fresh-brewed coffee.
I flash
back to my childhood. I am in the same
house. The same feelings flood
over me, take me back sixty years.

The Last Supper on the wall
Grandkids smile from the refrigerator door.

The house is still the same house.
At this table, the same table, in this kitchen,
I cut my quinceañera cake.

At this table in this house, the same house,
we sat talking after my father's death,
after Bueli's death,
after Tino's death, and
before
important events—
weddings, births, trips.

The legs of the table sustain us still.
Furniture is necessary context
for life in and out of doors.

Pat the windowsill.
Cry a tear of joy or sadness
in this house. The same house.
The very same house.
Our home.

MY MOTHER'S HANDS

Those hands. Her hands. I know them well. My mother's hands. Hands that wiped many a baby's bottom, hands that crocheted booties and hats and blouses and scarves, tablecloths and afghans. Those hands that rolled out thousands of flour tortillas, empanadas, piecrusts, tortillas de azúcar. Hands that lovingly caressed my father's face. That wiped a child's feverish forehead. That playfully patted a passing child's behind, maybe even raised a chancla to threaten a child acting all chiflado. Hands that massaged a colicky baby with olive oil. Hands that smacked a mosquito about to bite her baby and, equally adept, shooed away a fly from landing on her face. Hands espulgando a grandchild en las tardes de verano. Piojito. Or espulgando a beloved pet looking for pulgas or garrapatas. These are my mother's hands. In youth deftly applying lipstick. Now, gently but obsessively nervously twitching. Wrinkled and worn out, yet warm and loving. She holds out her hands. Mira que vieja estoy, she exclaims, surprised by the wrinkled skin, the liver spots, the twitch. At every good-bye, she expertly forms the cross with her thumb and index finger, touches my forehead, and blesses me: Que Diosito te bendiga.

LIVING IN DANGEROUS TIMES

I

We live in dangerous times.
Times that call for dangerous measures.
That call for witnessing and protesting.
Like we did in 1911 when they were lynching us
in South Texas. Brown bodies hanging from trees.
Like we did in 1972 when they were killing us
in the rice paddies of Vietnam and
the highways of Aztlán.
Raza must unite, cannot stand by
as they keep killing us, the poor,
the black
the brown
the ones who
cannot   will not
succumb.
We live in dangerous times.

II

We live in dangerous times.
Times that call for
dangerous tactics.
Tattooed body
piercings or body armor
cannot squelch the rising
peace of a serene and joyful heart.

III

Stop. Shoot. Die.
The heavy smell of gunpowder.
The sound of the gun reverberating in the heart.
The anxiety of not knowing—
is my child my husband my daughter my wife
asleep? Or dead?
Who are those on the evening news?
The maimed? The killed? Who are those
whose faces appear in the evening news?
Whose names I don't and do recognize.

IV

He walks into the casino in Monterrey.
Chaos reigns.
Charred remains lined against the wall.
On the red carpet the blood a darker red.

And then he sees the foot.
Her tiny foot, the one still wearing her black sandal.
The toe. He sees her toe. The single toe
he knows so well. He weeps.
"It's her. My wife.
She loved to play the slots,
las maquinitas.
We were to have dinner with our kids.
My three kids. Orphans, now.
We were to meet up for dinner
at the Chinese restaurant she liked so much."
He moans. Sollozando.
"She. My wife. A statistic now.
And I? De luto. No se que hacer.

¿Llorar? ¿Morir de dolor?
I can only remember her.
I will.
We will remember her."

VI

MEDITACIÓN FRONTERIZA

MEDITACIÓN FRONTERIZA
I, 2000

ESTA REALIDAD FRONTERIZA QUE NOS penetra hasta por los poros, con el polvo, el calor, los humos, olor a petróleo y a gardenia. Sí, esta realidad nos forja y nos hace lo que somos. El diario luchar por el pan de cada vida, de cada día, de cada vida, de cada día.

En esta frontera estoy atrapada. No, situada. No, desplegada. No, estacionada. No, aparcada. No, parqueada. No nada de atrapada o parqueada estoy como el río, siempre y nunca el mismo. Porque estoy haciendo cola para cruzar calmadamente, tranquila, con el calor sofocante, comiendo una raspa—o raspado—de mango que Pili me vendió hace dos cuadras, tranquila y legal no como los que se arriesgan con coyotes o a solas, no como los que vuelan como pájaros sin fronteras. Y sigo en mi Camry a vuelta de rueda como en el freeway en Houston during rush hour o en L.A. o en Monterrey pero mucho más lentamente, como en cámara lenta.

"Dame un dólar. ¿Sí?" Con sonsonete inocente la niña de seis o menos años con mano extendida susurra como mantra sagrada "Dame un dólar. ¿Sí?" Sus ojos café claro bajo cejas y pestañas negras color de chapapote clavados en los míos. Se llama América, su piel tostada por el vivir a la intemperie.

Y le doy una peseta y me da un chicle de la cajita que guarda como tesoro bajo el brazo. El olor a orines hostigamiento sin perdón hits me like a sudden migraine headache as we approach la iglesia donde hace más de cincuenta años me bautizo el padre Lozano. Sí el famoso padre Tomás Lozano que casó a mis padres y que todo mundo conoció y admiró y por quién todo mundo lloró cuando murió. La iglesia del Santo Niño—pero no el de Atocha. The churchyard is quiet under the hot sun. And we creep como hormigas bajo el sol que quema.

Un policía ¿sera municipal? de camisa blanca, European cut y pantalón azul, potbellied, as all good cops are wont to be, cobra su quota en la cantina el tal Ladies Bar Capricornio por Calle Ocampo. As I read the street name hand printed on the bluegreen wall of the bar, Ocampo, could it be Irish, O'Campo?

Sigo con paso lento y compro una imagen grandísima de la Virgen de Guadalupe del vendedor Epifanio de bigote grueso y negro, el de mi padre hace cuarenta años. Según Epifanio que lleva camiseta verde oscuro su padre las confecciona "allá por Toluca". La imagen de la morenita cópia laser fotostática a color con florecitas de tela blanca sobre azul enmarcada en madera sobredorada con spray paint que los chicos usan para ponerse locos. Yo y la Lupe seguimos a paso de tortuga—seguro aunque lento.

Las aguas del río Bravo Rio Grande del oeste vienen acarreando pedacitos de Nuevo México y de Colorado y de El Paso y de Eagle Pass—cachitos de tierras lejanas revueltos con cachos de mi corazón.

Del sur al norte cruzan turistas regresan a sus charter buses drunk and happy, cargados de plaster bulls, portando gigantescos sombreros de charros. También mujeres, jóvenes y viejas, que cruzan este domingo por la tarde de regreso a sus trabajos limpiando casas cuidando niños y ancianos. Negociantes con briefcases. Un grupo de chicanos de más al norte con sus pedacitos de México that they will display in dorm rooms, on visors, banderitas mexicanas para la fiesta del Cinco de Mayo en Wisconsin or Michigan.

Y del norte al sur vienen los mexicanos regresando a su tierra cargados de comestibles y necesidades de la vida, y gringos y otros que vienen a cenar cabrito al Rincón del Viejo o si no saben a cualquier restaurante por la avenida Guerrero. Chiveras con redes repletas de chucherías. Y chicanos buscando a piece of their soul who may end up en los brazos de una chica tan perdida tan joven como ellos en la Zona.

Y el río sigue su curso mágico hacia el mar donde se pierden las aguas of the Rocky Mountains in Colorado y los llanos de Nuevo México y los desperdicios de las maquiladoras de Ciudad Juárez las aguas de los ríos que corren y que llevan su verdad hasta el mar. ¿Y yo? Yo sigo mi paso, una más entre la multitud, pacientemente esperando el destino del rio, de la frontera, de esta cola en que me encuentro, el destino de mis países, de mi ser.

MEDITACIÓN FRONTERIZA
II, 2005

CRUZANDO DE UN LADO A otro siempre me lleva al pasado, a tantos cruces, a tantos viajes a Monterrey, visitando familiares, mamagrande, papagrande, tíos y tías, primos y primas. Amigas, amigos y familiares algunos tan lejanos que no se ni sus nombres. Al principio en tren— nicknamed La Marrana—que salía de Nuevo Laredo y pasaba por Villaldama y otros pueblos, hacia el sur. My maternal grandmother, Celia, would pack taquitos for our lunch, fruit and pan dulce for snacks. I learned to love trains, the lull of the wheels on the tracks. Since those early trips, I've traveled by train many times, in Europe and even in the United States, especially in the northeast.

Cuantas veces cruzaba ya de adulto íbamos a Nuevo Laredo a bailar en los clubs, Tony's y otros, y también in the '80s a un gay bar donde nunca me sentí a gusto, the thrill of being in a space that was dangerous. Bailando con mis amigos y regresando a Laredo a cenar en el Denny's a las dos o tres de la mañana, platicando de filosofía o de lo que nos había contado algún chavo de Méjico.

Post-NAFTA the border towns changed, are still changing. Walmart and H-E-B on the Mexican side are as crowded as the ones on the U.S. side. The small retailers closing shop and relocating to Laredo to try to salvage their businesses.

¿Cuándo? When will it end? This violence? This fear? This hate? Stifles life. Stifles art. Stifles.

La violencia se acuesta a dormir con la cotidianidad y se levanta tempranito. No sabemos de dónde viene ni a dónde va, pero sabemos que está siempre ahí, in our midst. En este mundo donde se encuentran muchos otros, solo los ángeles que andan desesperados y acongojados saben lo que yace en el corazón de quienes matan por matar. Y a los mismos ángeles se les cierra el mundo y no saben cómo responder. Y se ponen a llorar.

MEDITACIÓN FRONTERIZA
III, 2015

LIVING FAR FROM THE BORDER, I yearn for the smell of diesel gasoline, of carne asada and of gardenias. I yearn to hear the accordion, the radio stations with the distinctive Spanish of Nuevo Laredo and the Laredo Tejano Spanglish. The smells and sounds of that in-between space that is la frontera, my borderlands. I yearn to once again cross over to have dinner at La Victoria or El Rincón del Viejo, yet I know that even if I still lived there, I would not be crossing back and forth as we used to. I know that now, I would not be stalled in a long line waiting to cross back to Laredo after dinner or after an afternoon of shopping at La Frutería González and the Farmacia Benavides. Nowadays, my favorite restaurants from Nuevo Laredo can be found in Laredo, relocated because of the violence—La Única now sells delicious tostadas and flautas on the U.S. side. Others have closed altogether.

The people who need to still come and go, but most of us who crossed to have some fun, or for a meal or simply to visit friends, have stopped going. Too violent! Too risky. There's Joe, a salesman, who was held at knife point—they took his Tahoe. In plain daylight, too. Then there's David, the high-school math teacher, who got caught in a barricade; the cars all stopped and the thieves came car to car, scaring children and adults alike, stole wallets, watches, purses, and jewelry. No one was killed that time. We were lucky, David says. Now, his wife refuses to cross. Only funerals or weddings will draw Laredo families to cross together, and even then the relatives from Houston may be so fearful they stay away.

I attend a gathering of writers; we read our work, discuss our creative process, en la Casa de la Cultura—the old railroad station where I spent many hours waiting for the train, La Marrana, to take us to Monterrey some forty years ago. The young people who come to pick me up in Laredo, Texas, are confident and feel secure but don't take chances. Two poets, a novelist and a visual artist. The train station has been transformed. A beautiful art exhibit graces the walls. The literary gathering on one end. Art can save us. We believe it and trust that it is so. Still the killings, shootings, and beheadings continue. Poetry reigns, but the poetry of dead bodies suffocates. The young poets bring me back. I felt safe while in Nuevo Laredo, but once back in Laredo I feel a lump in my throat, my stomach contracts as a dozen or so young men roam the downtown streets as a group. I recognize this fear. I drive home, safe in my barrio home. How can one live with constant, quotidian fear?

The waters flow as they must, the river a witness to death and pain. The deforestation strips the riverbank so the reed cane that the matachines harvest for their nagüillas is gone. They use plastic drinking straws now to adorn their ceremonial dress. But more serious still, a crisis happens as the children come in droves from Honduras, San Salvador, all of Central America, hoping to be let in and allowed to stay. Fleeing the cartels, the violence of poverty, fleeing illness and hunger. So much to fear. They come to worse: the detention centers unprepared to care for them. The rumor is that the cartels are using the occasion to send killers to the United States, that they are recruiting and they are the ones spreading the misinformation. Who knows? Could be. The truth is that the kids are often sick and malnourished and need medical attention. But all need to be processed. Not just sent back. Yet they are sent back without even being processed or asked the right questions to determine if they qualify for asylum. Stories of persecution, of torture, of rapes, of threats of death sure and final. Here and everywhere the refugees come seeking safety, seeking dignity, seeking life. Seeking a future.

My border is no longer the tourist destination it was. The tourist money has dried up. The plazas lie deserted. Even residents dare not venture out after dark. It is too dangerous. Too risky. Too scary. The border has become a battleground. We are under siege.

All borders remain spaces of conflict, of violence; indeed, my border is a wound. But all over the world the wounds bleed, migrants flee the violence of war, military violence, flee drug cartel violence, the violence of poverty, of woman hating, of racism, of intolerance. All over the world those who can work work for a borderless world, a violence-free world. They dream an end to violence, dream of the tranquility of an accepting world. Dream the fulfillment of equality for all. Imagine, and it shall be so. Believe that it will be so.

ABOUT THE AUTHOR

A daughter of the borderlands, **Norma Elia Cantú** received her PhD in English from the University of Nebraska–Lincoln and has taught English and Chicanx studies at a number of institutions in Texas, California, Washington, D.C., and Missouri. She is the Norine R. and T. Frank Murchison Endowed Professor in the Humanities at Trinity University in San Antonio and professor emerita at the University of Texas at San Antonio. Cantú edits the Rio Grande/Río Bravo: Borderlands Culture and Traditions book series at the Texas A&M University Press and the Literatures of the Americas book series at Palgrave MacMillan. She has published articles on a number of academic subjects as well as poetry and fiction. Her publications on border literature, the teaching of English, quinceañera celebrations, and the matachines, a religious dance tradition, have earned her an international reputation as a scholar and folklorist. She has edited or co-edited eight books; published the novels *Canícula: Snapshots of a Girlhood en la Frontera* (University of New Mexico Press, 1995) and *Cabañuelas* (University of New Mexico Press, 2019); and collaborated with artist Marta Sánchez on *Transcendental Train Yard*.